YOU CAN save the planet

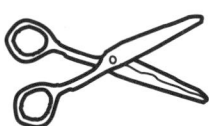

Luc

CONTENTS

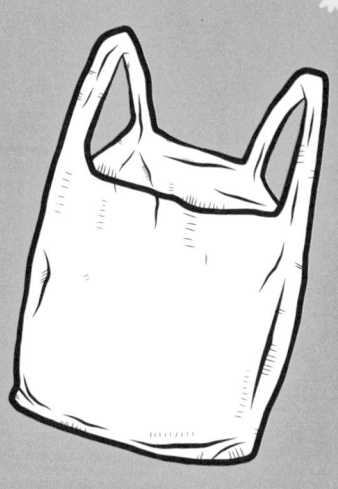

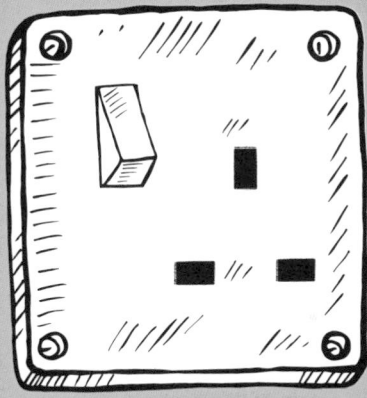

YOU CAN SAVE THE PLANET

Taking steps to save the planet is really important! This book will give you loads of inspiration so that YOU CAN go and start saving the planet today.

Everyone can do their bit to help the planet – no action is too small! This book is full of planet-saving tips and activities that can be done at home, at school, in town, in the countryside... you can help save the planet wherever you are!

There are activities for everyone – whether you want to make eco-friendly hair smoothies, plan car-free trips that are fun and keep you fit at the same time, or throw a plastic-free party to celebrate special occasions with your friends.

There are also plenty of spaces in the book for you to jot down your eco ideas, record the winners of team clean-ups and draw bike ride routes. So what are you waiting for? Read on, and then go and save the planet!

Earth is an incredible planet, home to amazing creatures, plants, beaches, rivers, streams, forests and mountains. There are so many animals in the world that we can't even count them – and humans share this planet with all of them.

But every day, problems are encountered that need to be fixed – litter in the park, plastic water bottles buried in the sand at the beach, bins overflowing in the street. The oceans are being polluted, thousands of animals are dying, and species are going extinct. Climate change is warming up the planet, melting icebergs and threatening animals and people.

Most people want to help resolve these problems but it's not always easy to know where to start. Some of the problems are so big that they can seem impossible for one person to change. But if everyone makes even one change, they can be fixed.

Now turn the page and start saving the planet!

SAVING THE PLANET STARTS HERE

If you love the Earth and want to save our planet, this book is for you. It contains information, ideas and activities to show you how to make simple changes that will make the Earth a safer, happier and greener place.

Taking your litter home is a great start.

* Start with the things that are easiest for you. You don't need to read this book in order – pick the activities you want to do most.

* Changing the world won't happen in a day, and you don't have to do everything at once. It's all about making a few changes at a time.

* Saving the planet is fun! Everyone is on their own journey to save the world, and every day something can be done to help.

* Remember to track your progress so you can see all the important changes you have made. Everything you do matters.

Track the things you've done to help save the planet.

Date	What I did to save the planet

FOOD FOR THOUGHT

There are so many yummy things to eat and drink. Hot, cold, spicy, sweet, strange, familiar – food is so good!

It's delicious, makes us feel content, and brings us all together at mealtimes. But it's also one of the main contributors when it comes to using plastic and generating waste.

Along with learning to cut down your plastic use and waste, it's important to make sure you're eating food that comes from a good place, was produced in an environmentally friendly way, and didn't cause anyone or anything to suffer.

CHOOSE 'HAPPY FOOD'

Food makes you happy, but not all food is made in a 'happy' way, so read on the next page about what to look for when you and your family are shopping.

* Eggs – make sure they are **free range**

* Meat – choose meat from an **ethical** source

* Fish – look for fish rated **green** on the 'Good Fish Guide'

9

HOW FAR HAS YOUR FOOD TRAVELLED?

One of the most important things about food is knowing where it comes from. Is it local, or did it have to travel hundreds of kilometres to get to you? The closer to home it was made, the fewer resources it took to transport it to you. The food will also be fresher!

Look at the labels on the items your family buys. Write down all the places that your food came from – each label should say 'Produce of…' or 'Made in…'. Now, are any of those things grown, made or produced in **this** country?

Write down 6 things that you could buy from local suppliers rather than from overseas ones.

1.

2.

3.

4.

5.

6.

VISIT A FARMERS' MARKET

If there's a farmers' market near you, go shopping there rather than at the supermarket.

You can be sure that the food is local. It could also be organic. And knowing where your food comes from can help you understand how it was grown and what it's made from. So ask the farmers about it – they'll be happy to tell you!

Most farmers' markets sell what's sometimes called 'ugly' fruit and vegetables. Incredibly, 40% of the fruit and vegetables produced in the UK is rejected by supermarkets because it doesn't look perfect, even though it still tastes the same. But does a wonky carrot really taste any different?

No! It's just as good as any other carrot. By buying 'ugly' produce, you're stopping these delicious fruits and vegetables from going to waste.

AT THE SHOPS

Single-use plastic shopping bags used to be free, but people used them without thinking. And they are terrible for the environment – they take 1000 years to break down and are a very obvious type of litter.

So a charge of 5p was introduced and it worked well. Before the charge was introduced, 7.6 billion plastic bags were used every year in England. Afterwards, that number fell to 1.75 billion.

However, these bags are still bad news, and it's much better to reuse bags or boxes. Here are some tips to remember.

* Always take a reusable bag with you when you go shopping.

* Say 'no, thank you' when a shop assistant goes to put your items in a plastic bag.

* Remind whoever you're shopping with to buy unpackaged fruit and vegetables – bring your own bags.

* And if you find yourself without a shopping bag, see how many potatoes you can carry!

GO ZERO-WASTE SHOPPING

Why not get rid of disposable packaging completely? 'Zero-waste' shops are becoming more and more common across the UK. You take your own reusable containers to these stores and fill them up to avoid plastic packaging.

Here are some of the alternative ways to take all your shopping home.

🌟 Fill little glass jars with dried herbs and spices.

🌟 Use large glass jars for dried store cupboard items like pasta and lentils.

🌟 Reuse glass bottles to store oils and vinegars.

🌟 You could reuse an old coffee tin to bring some more home.

🌟 Hessian and fabric bags can be used for potatoes and vegetables.

CHICKP...   PASTA   LENTILS

ECO-FRIENDLY LUNCH

Crisp bags, plastic sweet wrappers, metal drinks cans… they're all bad for the planet!

You can make your lunch eco-friendly – and healthy – by cutting out plastic packaging and waste.

Start by buying a stainless-steel lunch box, then go from there. A box with different compartments can be a great idea – that way you don't have to use wrapping to separate your food.

Here are some ideas to get you started.

- Eat food that comes in its own natural packaging, like bananas and apples. Fruit doesn't need to come in plastic – it's already wrapped! Remember to take your fruit scraps home to compost them.

- Avoid foods that are individually wrapped in soft plastics, such as sweets and chocolate bars.

- To reduce packaging, make your own muesli bars, biscuits or savoury muffins, and buy nuts in bulk.

- When you buy bread for your sandwiches, get it from a bakery and bring your own bag. You could even have a go at making your own bread!

Design your lunch box.

Yummy!

Try to avoid
too much
packaging.

When you've finished,
show it to a grown-up
and ask them to help
you make it for school.

USE WHAT YOU'VE GOT

When it comes to food, one of the most important things is to use what you've got. Before you buy more food, see if you can get creative and make something out of the things you have on hand, especially fruit and vegetables. Before you throw away (or compost) any old fruit and veg, see if you can use them in the recipes on the next few pages. Remember to ask a grown-up for help when using the stove or knives.

STOCK

Making stock is a great way to use all your old vegetables. Stock gives a flavour kick to soups, stews, sauces, pies and risottos.

What to do

1 Roughly chop all your vegetables and place them in a large saucepan. You don't even need to peel them! Add the herbs and bay leaves.

2 Add enough water to just cover all your ingredients.

3 Put the saucepan on the stove on a medium-high heat and bring to the boil.

4 Turn the heat down to low and allow to simmer for at least 1–2 hours. The longer the better!

5 Remove from the heat and strain the liquid into another saucepan or container.

6 Your stock can be stored in the fridge for 3–4 days, or frozen for 6 months.

You'll need:

* vegetables, such as onions, celery, carrots, turnips, leeks, parsnips and shallots

* herbs

* bay leaves

TIP!

Use a potato masher to crush your vegetables before straining your stock. This will give you loads of flavour from your ingredients. Just be careful – the liquid will be hot, so ask a grown-up to help!

HOMEMADE RECIPES

APPLE CRUMBLE

If your apples get too old to eat, you don't need to throw them away. A great way to use old apples, or a combination of fruits like pears, peaches, berries or plums, is to make a crumble. This one serves 5–6.

What to do

1 Preheat the oven to 180°C (gas mark 4).

2 Peel the apples (remember to put the peelings in your compost bin – see page 38), then roughly chop them into 1.5 cm cubes.

3 Place the apple cubes in a baking dish and toss with sugar, cinnamon and lemon juice.

4 To prepare the topping, mix all topping ingredients together in a bowl with your fingers until clumps form, then spread over the top of your apple mixture.

5 Bake for 30–40 minutes, or until the crumble is golden brown. Allow to stand for 10 minutes before serving.

6 Serve warm with vanilla ice cream.

You'll need:

Filling:

* 4 medium apples
* 100 g white sugar
* 1 teaspoon ground cinnamon
* 2 tablespoons lemon juice

Topping:

* 1 teaspoon cinnamon
* 100 g unsalted butter, melted
* 90 g rolled oats
* 120 g plain flour
* 135 g brown sugar

STRAWBERRY JAM

Jam is really easy to make, and an excellent way to use your leftover berries if they're starting to get too old to eat. And better yet, you can store your jam in a repurposed jar, and even give it as a gift!

You'll need:

* 500 g strawberries, leafy tops removed
* 350 g caster sugar
* ½ tablespoon lemon zest
* 1 tablespoon lemon juice
* 1 repurposed jam jar (sterilise by boiling in water for 10 minutes – ask a grown-up to help you)

What to do

1 Place the strawberries, caster sugar, lemon zest and juice in a saucepan and gently crush with a potato masher.

2 Place the saucepan on a low heat and simmer until the sugar dissolves. The sugar must be completely dissolved or your jam will not set correctly, and may have lumps of sugar.

3 Turn the heat up to medium–high and allow the mixture to boil rapidly for 10 minutes, stirring often. Use a long wooden spoon when stirring and watch out as boiling jam may spit.

4 Do the wrinkle test: spoon a little jam onto a cold plate, wait for 30 seconds, then push it with your finger. If the jam wrinkles up, it's ready, but if it spreads back out, keep boiling it for another 2 minutes or until the jam wrinkles when cooled.

5 Pour your jam into the jam jar and allow it to cool completely before sealing. Be very careful – the jam will be extremely hot! Ask an adult for help with this part. Store the jam in the fridge.

BE YOUR OWN FASHION DESIGNER

Holes in your jeans? Hoodie worn away at the elbows? T-shirt ripped? You could go and buy new ones. And everyone loves getting new things. But super-cheap clothes – known as 'fast fashion' – are really wasteful.

Repairing clothes is actually quite easy. Using a needle and thread, you can fix any tears or holes in your clothes and sew on new buttons. Also, you can use your creative skills to turn old clothes into something new, cool and totally unique.

For help with your sewing and fashion skills, ask a grown-up to help you look for 'upcycling' videos online.

DID YOU KNOW?

The fashion industry is the second biggest polluter in the world after the oil industry.

Think of three items that you could transform into something else.

* Jeans... into shorts.
* A hoodie into...
* A faded jacket into...
* A long skirt into...

KIDS WHO CHANGED THE WORLD

Maya Penn

One day, Maya found a piece of fabric lying in her house. Bursting with ideas, she used that piece of fabric to make a zebra-print headband decorated with a butterfly – the Zebra-Fly. Soon she began creating all sorts of accessories. When she wore them on the street, people gave her compliments, and asked if she had any for sale.

Aged just 8, Maya started her own business making eco-friendly clothes and accessories. She turned scraps of material into hats, scarves and bags. Her business quickly grew. She also helped other fashion brands become more sustainable and ethical.

Maya received a commendation from Barack Obama – President of the United States at the time – for her achievements in protecting the natural environment, and in 2016, she even had her first book, *You Got This!*, published. Everything starts with an idea!

GO ON A BARGAIN HUNT

Everyone could buy fewer items of clothing and make them last longer. But what do you do if you need new clothes, or just want to go clothes shopping for fun?

Fortunately, it's still possible to do this and help the planet – by going to charity shops instead. Get some friends together and go bargain hunting – there are many treasures to be found! You can often find very good-quality clothing brands for a much cheaper price.

And you'll probably come away with clothing that will last you a long time. Charity shops only sell clothing that is in good condition, and fast-fashion items often don't last long enough to be sold second-hand!

By shopping at charity stores, as well as donating your old things to them, you're keeping these items from ending up in landfill, while also helping a good cause.

Charity shops are also great places to pick up second-hand books, toys and games. Before you go, why don't you write or draw a list of bargains you'd like to get?

Microfibres are tiny fibres that can come out of your clothes in the wash. This is one way that plastic enters the food chain. By putting your clothes in a filter bag when you wash them, you can stop microfibres getting out.

My bargain hunt shopping list

THE GREAT GIVEAWAY

Buying things from charity and second-hand shops is a great idea. But where do the charity shops get their stock from in the first place?

From donations, by people just like you!

Go through your room and look for things that you really don't need any more. Could someone else love these items? Then you will be doing a good deed if you donate them to a charity shop.

TIP!

Don't just leave your donations outside the shop. Take them inside when it is open. The volunteers inside will be very happy to see you!

GET THE WHOLE FAMILY INVOLVED

Ever looked in a relative's wardrobe and thought, 'Wow, you have WAY too much stuff!'? Well, guess what, they probably have too! They have collected a lifetime's worth of stuff and there will definitely be some things in there that they no longer need, want or that fit.

So, suggest that you go through their wardrobes with them and set aside items to give to charity.

Remind them that the clothes are going to live again, making someone else happy and earning money for a worthy cause.

GIVE YOUR OLD CLOTHES A SECOND LIFE

Ever grow out of clothes before you wear them out? No wonder – you're growing fast! So what do you do with these old clothes? Maybe you pass them on to your younger siblings. But if that isn't the case, why don't you give them to a kid who would be super glad to have them?

There are charities such as **www.marysmeals.org.uk** that will send your clothes and other goodies to some of the poorest children in the world.

How you can help

* It all starts with a backpack (perhaps last year's school bag if you got a new one this year).

* Then you fill the backpack with clothes and other useful items.

* You give it to the charity and they ship it to some of the world's poorest communities, and give it to a child who could really use it there.

Here's a checklist of what you could pack:

- ☐ Clothes for kids aged 4–12, such as shorts, skirts, T-shirts and dresses
- ☐ Flip-flops or sandals
- ☐ Notepad
- ☐ Pencils, crayons
- ☐ Eraser, ruler, sharpener, pencil case
- ☐ Towel
- ☐ Soap, toothbrush, toothpaste
- ☐ Small ball
- ☐ Spoon

PLAN A FAMILY BIKE ADVENTURE

Next time someone suggests driving somewhere for a day out, go on your bikes instead.

If you drive 15 km on a day trip, your car will give out almost 5 kg of carbon dioxide. Carbon dioxide is a 'greenhouse gas' – it can trap heat in the Earth's atmosphere. Too much carbon dioxide in the atmosphere could lead to dangerous global warming.

Car exhausts also include other pollutants – gases and particles that poison the air and damage people's lungs.

Your bike, however, gives out no pollution at all! Cycling also helps keep you fit, gets you out into nature and is simply great fun. So, plan a bike adventure today.

Plan your route

✳ Mark out your route on a paper map using a pencil.

✳ Or plot your route using Google Maps. If you click the 'Cycling' icon, you can plot a bike-friendly route. It even shows your route's elevation (how much up and down there is) so you can make sure no one gets too puffed out!

✳ Remember to pack a hearty lunch – you'll need the energy. And everyone should definitely have a reusable water bottle.

Draw or describe your bike ride route here.

GO ON A STAYCATION

Flying off to a foreign country is a fantastic adventure. But if you're thinking about all that jet fuel being burned up in the atmosphere, then why not choose a holiday with less environmental impact. How about a vacation where you stay closer to home – a staycation!

There are so many exciting and adventurous places to go that are right on your doorstep: history-packed cities, fun beaches, and the wild and wonderful countryside.

Why not go to your local library and borrow a travel guide about Britain? You'll be amazed how much there is to discover just around the corner.

VISIT ALL THE NATIONAL PARKS

National Parks are areas of exceptional natural beauty that are specially protected. There are 15 National Parks in the UK. They are full of magical scenery, wonderful wild creatures and exciting things to do. Why don't you visit them all? Tick off each park below once you've visited it.

You could even start your adventure today by visiting **nationalparks.uk**

I have been to all these National Parks:

- ☐ Brecon Beacons
- ☐ Broads
- ☐ Cairngorms
- ☐ Dartmoor
- ☐ Exmoor
- ☐ Lake District
- ☐ Loch Lomond and The Trossachs
- ☐ New Forest
- ☐ Northumberland
- ☐ North York Moors
- ☐ Peak District
- ☐ Pembrokeshire Coast
- ☐ Snowdonia
- ☐ South Downs
- ☐ Yorkshire Dales

WALK TO SCHOOL

If everybody in your class got driven to school, that would be up to 30 separate car journeys and 30 exhaust pipes pumping out nasty fumes. That's bad for the planet and for your lungs.

If you live quite close to school, why not talk to a grown-up about walking there? It will save on car fuel and it's a brilliant way to start the day. The walk will wake you up and put you in a good frame of mind for the day.

You could meet up with your classmates on the way and all walk together. What would be the best route to take?

TIP!

There is no such thing as bad weather, only badly chosen clothing! So just because it's raining, you can still walk to school. Just pull on your wellies, a waterproof coat, warm gloves and take an umbrella.

Why don't you draw a map of your route here?

GET YOUR RUBBISH SORTED

Have you ever wondered where all your rubbish goes? If it isn't recycled, your rubbish gets taken to a landfill. It is literally thrown into a big hole in the ground.

Unfortunately, landfills pollute the environment, contaminate groundwater and soil, threaten wildlife, and produce greenhouse gases like methane and carbon dioxide.

That's why it's so important that we reduce the amount of rubbish we produce, reuse items and recycle things whenever possible.

DID YOU KNOW?

Every day, the average UK family creates nearly 2.5 kilos of waste. Over one year, that's enough waste to fill a 3-bedroom house!

REDUCE, REUSE, RECYCLE

Most people are confused about what they can and can't recycle, so here's a quick guide. You can put the following items in your kerbside recycling bin:

- hard plastic
- glass
- cardboard
- paper
- metal and cans (including aluminium cans, deodorant and hairspray cans)
- milk and juice cartons

Things to remember:

- Make sure containers are empty.
- Both jars and their lids can be recycled, but keep them separate when putting them in your kerbside bin.
- Keep items loose, not bundled together inside other items like bags or boxes.

TEAM CLEAN-UP

Have you ever gone for a walk to a beautiful spot and seen lots of horrible litter? So nasty!

You could make a difference – and have fun at the same time.

What to do

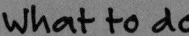

1 Pick a spot that needs a clean-up. This could be your local park, woods, a river, canal or beach.

2 Get some volunteers. Ask your friends, neighbours and family.

3 Agree a time and place to meet.

4 Start picking up litter!

5 Reward yourselves with a treat.

You'll need:
- gloves
- litter pickers
- welly boots
- bin bags
- friends
- a grown-up to take the litter to the tip

Are your friends competitive? Why not turn your clean-up into a challenge?

OUR AWESOME CLEAN-UP CHALLENGE

Where: _____

Date: _____ Time: _____

Team A

Name: _____

Members: _____

Number of bags filled: _____

Team B

Name: _____

Members: _____

Number of bags filled: _____

Winners:

_____

_____

Of course, nature is the big winner!

MAKE A COMPOST BIN

More than half of the rubbish in household bins is food scraps. Food scraps in landfill are one of the main causes of harmful greenhouse gases.

By putting your food scraps in a compost bin instead, you can significantly reduce the food waste you and your family send to landfill. Composting also creates soil that is rich in nutrients, which you can use in your garden to make your plants grow.

CARBON AND NITROGEN

The best compost has a good balance of carbon (brown) and nitrogen (green) – about 3:1. Carbon and nitrogen are the magic ingredients in nature that help the microorganisms (like bacteria and fungi) digest your compost.

Green layers include: fresh grass clippings, clippings from plants with leaves, fruit and vegetable scraps, and coffee grounds.

Brown layers include: dead leaves, straw, hay, twigs, shredded newspaper and cardboard.

TIP!

Every time you add a green layer to your compost, add some brown over the top. This will help your compost decompose.

HOW TO MAKE A COMPOST BIN

1 Decide where you're going to set up your compost bin – ideally, this should be somewhere dry and shady, where you can easily access water.

2 Find something to use as your compost bin. Old rubbish bins and wooden boxes can work well. You can also set aside a patch of dirt surrounded by a ring of chicken wire if you have space outside.

3 Add a few brown and green layers (see 'Carbon and nitrogen' opposite) to get your compost started – try layering: brown, water, brown, green, brown, water, green, brown, and make your brown layers about three times as thick as your green layers.

4 Add water as often as needed to keep your compost moist, but not too wet.

5 Use a spade to turn your pile once a week, moving the bottom layers up to the top. This helps mix air through your compost to keep it healthy.

6 That's it! Keep an old ice-cream container or small bucket in your kitchen so you can throw all your scraps into it. Empty this into your compost each day.

7 It can take anywhere from 3–12 months for the scraps you put in your compost to finish decomposing. You'll know when they're done because they will be dark and rich in colour, and you won't be able to see any of the original materials.

REPURPOSE AND REUSE

Apart from food and kitchen scraps, there are lots of things that we throw away without even thinking – how many can you think of?

Here are just a few examples of ways you can reuse these things. You can probably come up with lots of other ways.

GLASS JARS can be used to organise any small items you have, or they make pretty decorations if you fill them with pebbles or shells. Make a windproof candle using a glass jar, or use them to store homemade jams.

EGG CARTONS can be used to sprout seedlings, to sort your jewellery or other small items, or can be donated to local farmers or anyone you know with chickens.

OLD OR OUTGROWN CLOTHING can be cut into rags to use for cleaning. Use thicker items like jeans or corduroy garments to make patches to repair your other clothes.

NEWSPAPER AND SCRAP PAPER can be used to line bins or used as the bottom layer of a garden bed.

ICE-CREAM STICKS AND WOODEN SPOONS can be used as plant markers – write the names of your herbs and flowers on them.

REPURPOSING A SPRAY BOTTLE

There are lots of ways you can reuse an empty spray bottle. Choose a spray bottle that didn't contain any chemicals then wash it out. Also, keep your bottles for household and personal care separate. Then try the following fabulous uses.

HYDRATING MIST

Fill your spray bottle with ⅓ purified water and ⅔ rosewater, then add a few drops of chamomile essential oil (ask a grown-up to help you find these items in big supermarkets or pharmacists). Spray onto your face and skin for a refreshing, cooling mist.

AIR FRESHENER

Simply mix water and a few drops of your favourite essential oils in your empty spray bottle, and then get spritzing!

HOUSEHOLD CLEANER

Fill a large spray bottle with ½ water, ½ white vinegar and 10 drops of eucalyptus or tea tree oil. You can use this all around the house and in the bathroom to make everything fresh and clean.

PLASTIC NOT FANTASTIC

The number of plastic items on Earth is in the trillions. There are more than 5 trillion pieces of plastic in the oceans alone. That is a huge number!

With 5 trillion teaspoons of water, you could fill over 9800 Olympic swimming pools. And if you joined all of those pieces of plastic together, they would go around the whole planet more than 4000 times.

Plastic contains chemicals that are harmful to humans. Animals often mistake small bits of plastic for food and feed them to their young, who can choke on them or become sick.

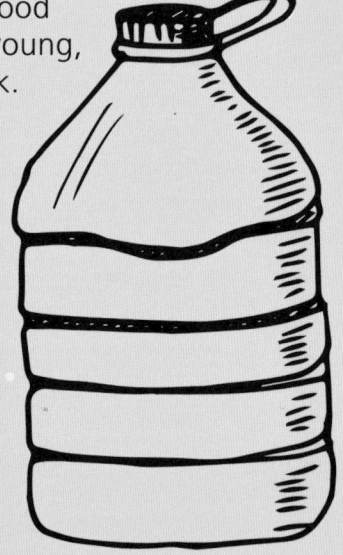

Getting rid of the plastic in our lives is almost impossible. But cutting back a little bit can make a big difference. Every time you choose an alternative to plastic, you're helping to save an animal, save the oceans and stop the spread of toxic chemicals, making the world a happier place.

A lot of toys are made from plastic, and while they're lots of fun, you probably won't use them forever. Have a go at sorting your toys into those that are made from plastic and those that aren't.

Work out which toys are your favourites and look after them so you don't need to throw them away and get new ones. When your toys break, see if you can fix them instead of throwing them away, and if you really don't need them anymore, donate them to charity.

Or you could use bits of old toys to create a piece of art or a new toy!

WATER BOTTLES

The water in your tap is perfectly good to drink – so why do we buy so many plastic water and drinks bottles?

Bottled water first became popular in the 1980s. At the time, no one actually believed people would pay for bottled water when they could get it for free. But incredibly, they did!

Now, each year, people in the UK buy 7.7 billion plastic water bottles. Sadly, only 1 in 3 of those bottles are recycled. But that can be improved!

Instead of buying your water in a plastic bottle, get a reusable water bottle, such as a stainless-steel bottle. These are available in a range of colours, sizes and patterns, and will last you a long time. Alternatively, you can start by reusing bottles you already own. Think before you drink!

FACT!

Every minute, more than 1 million bottles of water are bought worldwide.

TIP!

You can also buy reusable milkshake and juice cups, which you can take to cafés or fill with your own homemade drinks.

CUT DOWN ON COFFEE CUPS

It's time to get adults to think before they drink, too. Have you ever been out in town and been amazed at how many people are drinking from takeaway coffee cups? They're everywhere!

But now many coffee shops give you a discount if you bring your own cup. So the reusable cup soon makes money sense as well as eco sense!

Right, it's time to test your maths skills. Fill in this quiz, show it to a grown-up, and see if they get the message.

1 A latte costs £1.80. Bring your own cup and you get 20p off. How much would your latte cost?

_____

_____

2 A reusable cup costs £1. But every time you use it you save 25p. How many coffees will you need to buy before the cup is paid for by the discount?

_____

_____

3 A filter coffee costs 99p. They give you 50p off with your own cup. How much would your filter coffee cost?

_____

_____

PLASTIC-FREE PARTY

Birthday parties are tons of fun, but they can use **a lot** of plastic. Try these ideas for a planet-friendly plastic-free party. They can also make your party unique, and even more special.

* Send your party invitations by email, or send your guests a packet of seeds with a note telling them to bring the seeds to plant at your party.

* Use your own plates and glasses, or ask your friends to bring their own.

* Use old jam jars for drinks, instead of plastic cups.

* Put natural beeswax candles on your cake.

* Use paper instead of plastic bags for your party bags. Or, instead of party bags, give each guest a pot and some seeds to grow their very own pot plant.

* Plastic-free party activities could include tie-dyeing a T-shirt or socks, pottery-making, playing hide and seek or musical chairs.

THINGS TO AVOID:

glitter, party poppers and blowers, confetti, plastic party bags, single-use plastic tablecloths and banners, and plastic plates, cups and cutlery.

DESIGN YOUR OWN PARTY DECORATIONS

Instead of using balloons as party decorations, try things like tissue-paper pompoms, streamers, origami, kites, tea lights or solar fairy lights. Or use things from nature, like flowers in repurposed jars, leaves, pebbles, stones and shells. You can also have your party outdoors, where nature is your decoration.

How will you decorate your party in a green way?

SAY BYE-BYE TO STRAWS

Straws are a fun way to enjoy a drink – for you. But that little burst of bubbles on your tongue can be no fun at all for sea creatures. In fact, straws can be deadly.

Many straws end up in the sea where animals eat them, thinking they are food. This makes them very sick or even kills them.

In Britain 5 billion plastic straws are used every year. Each of these straws takes more than 200 years to break down. That means the straws you use today will still be around when your great-great-great-great-great-grandchildren are alive.

So next time you get a drink or a milkshake in a café, just ask for no straw.

If you really want to keep using straws, here are some things you could try instead. Just remember to take them with you:

* metal straws, which you can clean and reuse
* bamboo straws, which are also reusable
* paper straws

100,000 marine creatures and around 1 million sea birds die each year from plastic entanglement.

DO I REALLY NEED IT?

One of the biggest steps in reducing the number of things you throw away is to buy less. And one of the easiest ways to buy less is to avoid going to shopping centres unless you really need to.

Whenever you are about to buy something made of plastic, ask yourself:

- Do I actually need to buy this?
- Can I buy an alternative product that's not made of plastic?
- If I really need it, is there a way I can reuse the plastic once I'm finished with it?

DO SOMETHING FUN INSTEAD

Try not to make shopping an activity that you do with your friends. Being surrounded by new and exciting things can make it hard to resist buying them. Instead, try to think of all the things you already own, and to find other ways you can use them. If you do have to go to the shops, write a firm list of everything you need, and only buy what's on the list.

Shopping list (Only things I REALLY need)

Then, instead of going shopping, plan a fun outdoors activity with your friends. Here are a few ideas – why don't you think of some more?

1. Build a tree swing
2. Bury treasure and draw a map
3. Go on a bike ride
4.
5.
6.

IN THE BATHROOM

Look around your bathroom at all the plastic things –
toothbrushes, toothpaste tubes, dental floss, containers for
shower gel, shampoo, conditioner, lip balm and deodorant,
combs and hairbrushes, plastic razors, cotton buds, soap packets,
bath toys, maybe even a shower curtain. The list seems never-
ending, doesn't it?

Start by changing just one thing at a time, and do your research –
there are plastic-free alternatives to most of these products.

Shower gel is really just liquid soap in a plastic bottle, so why
not simply use a bar of soap? You can further cut down on the
amount of plastic you buy by using bar shampoo instead of
shampoo in plastic bottles.

Write a list of 5 things in your bathroom that
you are going to change for something more
eco-friendly.

1.

2.

3.

4.

5.

BAMBOO TOOTHBRUSHES

A bamboo toothbrush is a great alternative to a plastic one. They brush your teeth just as well as plastic ones, but when they wear out, you can put them in your composting bin.

FACT!

Toothbrushes are one of the top ten items found in coastal clean-ups.

BATHROOM RECIPES

Try the following recipes, or come up with some of your own using natural ingredients.

BANANARAMA HAIR SMOOTHIE

This sweet conditioner will leave your hair looking sleek and shiny. Bananas contain potassium, natural oils and vitamins, which help protect your hair. Olive oil repairs damaged hair and prevents dandruff. Honey seals moisture into your hair and also contains beneficial antioxidants. This conditioner is so natural, it's almost good enough to eat!

You'll need:

* 1 mashed banana
* 1 tablespoon olive oil
* 2 tablespoons honey (it's best to use local organic)

What to do

Mix all the ingredients together thoroughly until smooth, then apply evenly to damp hair. Wait for 10–15 minutes then rinse well. Use 1–2 times a week.

LAVENDER BATH SALTS

For a relaxing and luxurious bath that's great for your muscles – especially if you've been doing activities like sport – try making your own bath salts instead of buying products that come in plastic. The Epsom salt in bath salts is made of magnesium sulfate, which can be absorbed through the skin to relieve muscle pain. It's even thought to help heal cuts.

You can experiment with different types of essential oils, herbs and dried flowers to make your salts. Bath salts also make a great gift, and you can decorate the repurposed jar!

You'll need:

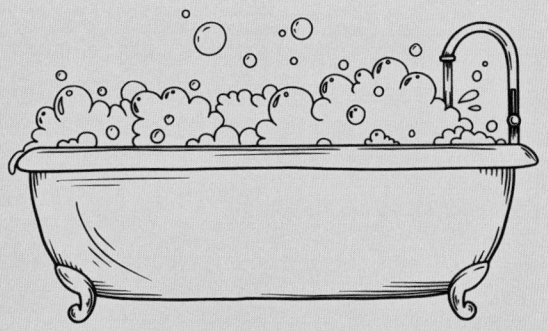

* 2 cups Epsom salt

* ¼ cup Himalayan rock salt

* 2 tablespoons coconut oil

* 10–15 drops lavender essential oil (available from most chemists and supermarkets)

* Optional: dried lavender, dried rosebuds, 2 tablespoons chamomile or mint tea, herbs from your garden

What to do

Mix all the ingredients together in a large bowl, then store in a sealable glass jar, such as an old jam or honey jar. Use about ¼ cup of salts in each bath.

USE LESS ELECTRICITY

Electricity is often taken for granted – it can be easy to forget that we're lucky to have access to power whenever we need it. But energy production causes toxic fumes and greenhouse gases, and most forms of electricity production use up the Earth's natural resources, such as trees, coal and natural gas.

Saving energy starts at home. With a few simple changes, you can help make the planet healthier and look after its future... and reduce your home's electricity bill!

TURN OFF THE LIGHTS

Every time you leave a room, make sure to turn the light off behind you. (But if someone shouts 'Hey!', you might need to turn it back on again.)

START UNPLUGGING

Did you know that when charging cables are plugged into power points, they can still use energy – even if they're not plugged into the item they're supposed to be charging? Turn off power points when they aren't being used and unplug phone chargers when they're not in use.

Top tips for cutting down your energy use

1 Read a book in the sunshine instead of watching TV inside.

2 Don't be scared of the dark; you can see the stars better when the lights are off.

3 Put on a jumper and cuddle your cat or dog or bunny or guinea pig instead of turning the heater on.

4 If you have a heater or air conditioner on, keep the doors and windows closed tight!

5 Don't open and close the fridge all the time (unfortunately, it doesn't make yummy food appear and it wastes energy).

What are your electricity saving ideas?

Write down 3 ways you could save electricity in your house, and show them to your family.

1. _____

_____

2. _____

_____

3. _____

_____

HIPPO HAPPINESS

Water is precious.

Everyone knows it's important to flush the toilet after you use it. But most toilets flush more water than the job needs!

Modern toilets use around 3 litres of water each time. Older toilets can use **14 litres** per flush!

FACT!

There are 27 million houses in Britain, and lots of them are old. That means BILLIONS of litres of water are wasted every day.

Got a calculator?

★ How many times do you flush the toilet each day?

★ Multiply that by the number of people in your family.

★ Multiply that by 14 litres per flush.

★ Multiply that by 27 million

= _____ billion litres just flushed away.

TIME TO PUT A HIPPO IN YOUR HOUSE

If you have an older toilet, you can easily reduce the amount of water you flush. All you have to do is put a hippo in your toilet's cistern!

Not a real hippo, obviously (it would be a bit of a squeeze) – a mini-hippo – okay, a stone!

The stone (or brick) takes up space in your cistern so that less water is flushed each time.

What to do

* Go on a walk in the country, to the beach or to a local river.

* Find a nice hippo-shaped rock about 20 cm long by 15 cm across.

* Take your rock home and draw a hippo's face onto it with a marker pen. (Hippos love wallowing in water, but you could draw anything you want.)

* Ask a grown-up to open your toilet's cistern lid. It's usually quite simple.

FACT!

Your toilet's water tank is called a 'cistern'.

* Place the hippo in the bottom of the cistern, under the flushing mechanism.

* Now every single flush will save around 3 litres of water.

* **Super important** – tell the person paying the water bill you are also saving them over **£20 a year**!

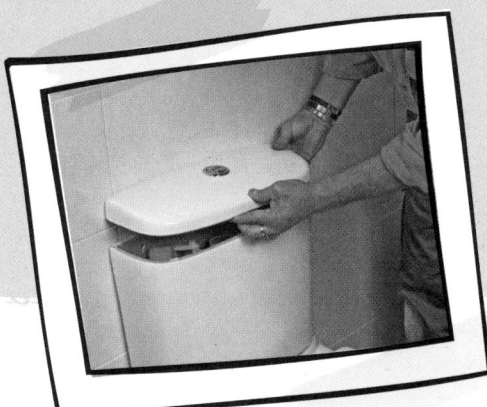

DESIGN AN ECO-FRIENDLY HOUSE

Okay, so you know about some ways to save energy. Now, how could you build that into your ideal house? Some architects have designed houses that are very easy to keep warm and that don't use much energy. Could you do better?

Think about:

⁕ what to use for the roof and walls

⁕ the design of the windows

⁕ energy saving gadgets

⁕ recycling ideas

⁕ the location of your house

Ask a grown-up to help you research some other ideas online.

Draw and label your dream eco house here.

BIG LITTLE ENERGY IDEAS

There are lots of ways that you can save energy and water. Each one might only help a little bit, but if you do them every day from now on, they will add up to a big saving. Imagine if you got your friends and family to follow them as well...

- Turn off lights when you're not in the room.

- Turn off the tap when you're brushing your teeth.

- Turn down your thermostat. Half of your home energy goes on heat and hot water. Turning the heating down by just one degree could save £80 a year.

- Wash clothes at 30 degrees rather than 40 degrees, or you could even wash them in cold water.

- Bye-bye standby. Turn your electronic devices such as TVs and computers completely off when not in use. Standby mode still uses energy!

- Have shorter showers. Cut your time in the shower by just 2 minutes and you could save more than 16 litres of water.

Now you've tried these suggestions, why not think of some more of your own?

My top energy and water saving ideas

1.

2.

3.

4.

5.

6.

7.

PLANT A TREE

Planting a tree is easy to do and a great way to give back to Mother Nature.

The tree you plant could live for hundreds or even a thousand years! Who knows, maybe one day YOUR children could climb it or build a treehouse in its branches!

What to do

1 Choose your planting site. Your tree will need lots of space to grow.

2 Dig a hole 2 to 3 times the diameter of the tree's root ball and deep enough to hold the soil and root ball.

3 Remove the tree from the pot and place it in the hole.

4 Cover the root ball with loose soil.

5 Thoroughly soak the tree with several large watering cans of water.

6 Water it well once a week if the weather is dry.

7 Track your tree's growth by taking regular photos.

You'll need:

✳ a native tree sapling (a young tree), such as oak, beech, Scots pine, maple, holly, silver birch or hazel (go with a grown-up to buy one from your local garden centre)

✳ adult- and kid-sized shovels and gardening gloves

✳ a large watering can

START A GARDEN

One of the best ways to enjoy nature and help change the world is to start your own garden. Whether you live in a house or a flat, there are ways for you to start growing things.

Starting an outdoor garden

1 Try to find a spot that gets at least 5 hours of sunlight every day. If this isn't possible, ask at your garden centre for plants that like shade. Also keep in mind that you'll need regular access to water so try to choose a spot that's near a hose or tap.

2 Mark out the area for your garden bed. Make it no wider than 120 cm, so you can always reach the middle of your garden without stepping on the plants.

3 Prepare the soil using a spade and a pitchfork to turn the grass over and loosen up the dirt. This will give you better drainage.

4 Cover the turned earth with a few sheets of wet cardboard, hay or cloth. Keeping these materials wet will ensure that moisture isn't sucked out of the soil.

5 Line the perimeter of your garden. You can use rot-resistant wooden boards, logs or bricks, or get creative and use rocks to mark the area.

6 Fill your bed with a combination of soil and compost.

7 After you've put your plants in, you can also cover your garden bed with mulch (a layer of something such as old leaves, or manure) to keep those pesky weeds away, help maintain moisture and protect your soil.

Plan your garden in this space.

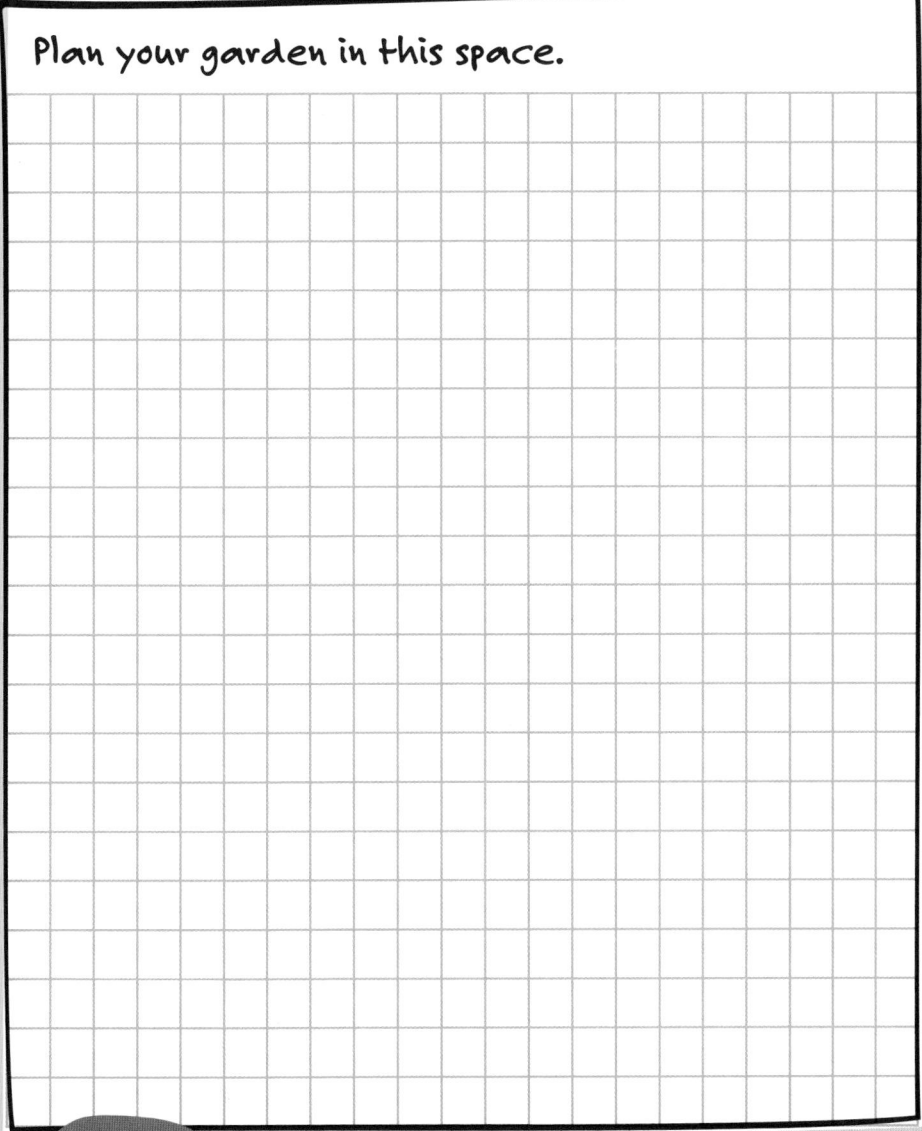

TIP!

If you want to grow edible plants, aim for a spot that gets morning sun and afternoon shade.

CREATE A
BALCONY GARDEN

If you live in a flat, a balcony garden is a brilliant way to bring some green space to your home. You can even grow your own food!

It's important to choose plants that are right for the kind of sunlight you get on your balcony. You might want to spend a few days watching how much sun your balcony gets throughout the day.

Choose the biggest pots that you have space for. The more soil the pots hold, the more moisture they will hold, and this will stop your plants drying out. Always buy pots that have drainage holes, then place the pots in a tray or line the bottom with cloth so the soil doesn't spill out. You can also get hanging pots that go on hooks, or pots that can hook onto the railing of your balcony.

Buy potting mix from your local nursery, and don't forget to add in your extra-good compost mix if you have some – your plants will love it.

HOME-GROWN FLAVOURS

Herbs grow well in pots, and so do many types of flowers, fruits and veggies. Here are some of the easiest plants to grow in pots (but remember to check how much sunlight you get!):

* **HERBS:** rosemary, mint, parsley and chives

* **FRUIT / VEG:** lettuce and salad leaves, cucumbers, tomatoes, strawberries, dwarf citrus trees

* **FLOWERS:** marigolds, lavender, geraniums, begonias

* **SUCCULENTS (plants which have thick, fleshy leaves):** all succulent species, but especially aloe vera

Watering is super important. One of the main reasons balcony plants die is lack of water. Unless your balcony plants get plenty of rain, you will need to water them pretty much every day. Just remember, different plants like different amounts of moisture, so check how much water your plants need.

GROW A GARDEN INDOORS WITH MICROGREENS

You don't even need outdoor space to start your own garden. Microgreens are seeds growing in soil that have burst open, become green and developed their first leaves. They are the next stage of a plant after they have sprouted.

Microgreens are extremely healthy – you can use them to garnish your dinner, eat them in salads, put them on pizza, put them on Marmite or avocado on toast, or just add them to a sandwich. You can eat them with pretty much anything!

A great way to reuse clear plastic containers from buying berries or cherry tomatoes is to grow microgreens and sprout herbs. You just need access to good light, like a windowsill, or a table near a glass door.

You'll need:

- ✳ organic seeds such as basil, beets, broccoli, cabbage, celery, coriander, kale, lettuce, mustard, parsley, peas, radish, rocket, spinach and many others
- ✳ a repurposed plastic punnet
- ✳ soil from your compost, local garden centre or hardware store
- ✳ a repurposed spray bottle
- ✳ scissors

What to do

1 Prepare your seeds by soaking them in warm water for a couple of hours.

2 Meanwhile, fill your plastic punnet about ¾ full with soil. Add a little water to the soil to make it moist. Put the punnet on a plate to stop soil and water leaking.

3 When your seeds have finished soaking, sprinkle them over the soil, then cover them with a small amount of dry soil. The covering only needs to be about half a centimetre deep.

4 Once seeds start sprouting, lightly mist your plants regularly to keep the soil moist but not too wet. You can close the punnet lid to keep the air nice and humid for your seeds to grow.

5 When your seedlings are anywhere from 2.5 to 10 cm tall, use scissors to cut the stems just above the soil. They're ready to eat!

BEE-FRIEND THE BEES

Bees are amazing – they are one of the hardest-working creatures on the planet! If they didn't exist, the world would be in big trouble.

Bees play an important role in pollinating all sorts of fruits and vegetables, as well as crops that are used to feed livestock. But sadly, native bee populations are under threat. Their natural habitats are being lost to urban developments that don't have enough trees and flowers to keep the bees alive. They are also disappearing due to pesticide use and disease.

WHAT IS POLLINATION?

Pollination is when the pollen from the male part of the plant is transferred to the female part of the plant. This makes new seedlings. Bees fly from flower to flower, and when they land, pollen sticks to their legs. When they land on the next plant, they transfer the pollen and help the plant.

FACT!

1 in every 3 bites of food eaten comes from plants that are pollinated by bees.

HELP THE BEES

You can help the bees by growing plants they love. These include:

FLOWERS lavender, daisies, marigolds, roses, foxgloves, nasturtiums, geraniums, clover, sunflowers

HERBS rosemary, basil, mint, thyme, parsley, fennel, coriander, oregano, sage

BERRIES strawberries, raspberries, blueberries

If you REALLY want to help the bees, you could ask for a beehive for your birthday! Bee-keeping is a fascinating hobby. Plus, everyone loves honey!

DID YOU KNOW?

The most bee-friendly flowers are usually yellow, blue and purple.

ADOPT AN ANIMAL

Do you like wild animals? Would you like to help protect some of the world's most vulnerable creatures?

A great way to do this is to adopt an animal through a charity.

DO I REALLY ADOPT THEM?

They don't come and live in your house, if that's what you're thinking! You make a donation to the animal charity and they send you information about a particular animal. The animal will be from an endangered species. The money you give is a huge boost to the charity's work. It could help them reduce poaching, protect their habitat or establish a safe reserve for the animals.

In return you often get a gift pack telling you all about the animal, regular updates on what's happening in your animal's world and a soft toy!

You can do all this for around £3 per month. That's the cost of a few bags of sweets. You could save that from your pocket money, do some chores for cash or make something to sell.

Check out **bornfree.org.uk** and **wwf.org.uk** for more information.

Which animal would you like to adopt?

* amur leopard
* dolphin
* elephant
* giant panda
* gorilla
* jaguar
* lion
* orangutan
* penguin
* polar bear
* snow leopard
* tiger
* turtle

MAKE THE BIRDS FEEL AT HOME

A bird feeder is a brilliant way to bring nature to your doorstep. It's also a big help to our feathered friends when there isn't much food around.

You can easily make one with an old plastic bottle!

Different birds appear in UK gardens at different times of year, but there will always be some hungry birds on the hunt for a snack.

What to do

1 Wash out the bottle and remove the cap. Make several small drainage holes in the base of the bottle with the pin.

2 Use scissors (carefully!) to make two level holes on opposite sides of the bottle near the bottom.

3 Slide a stick through these holes. You need around 5 cm of stick outside the bottle on each side to form perches.

4 Cut feeding holes in the bottle above the perches.

5 Cut holes near the neck of the bottle for the string.

6 Fill your bottle with seed mix (this is easier with a funnel) and screw on the cap.

7 Hang your feeder from a branch or washing line.

8 It may take the birds a few days to notice their new snack bar. Once they do, you can identify different species and photograph them.

You'll need:

- a repurposed plastic bottle (with cap)
- a stick
- a pin
- scissors
- string

SAVE THE ORANGUTANS

There's an ingredient that you probably use every day that is very bad news for orangutans – palm oil. 90% of palm oil comes from Indonesia and Malaysia. The problem is that the palm trees it comes from are home to orangutans. So much palm oil is being made that orangutans are being left with nowhere to live and are now a critically endangered species. Something needs to be done before these amazing creatures are lost forever. Let's cut out palm oil!

By avoiding palm oil, you help reduce the demand for it, which slows down the destruction of the orangutans' homes.

DO THE PALM OIL PUZZLE

The first step in cutting down your palm oil use is to check how much of it you use.

You and your family probably use lots of these things. Tick the ones you think are often made with palm oil.

- ☐ Bread
- ☐ Shampoo
- ☐ Lollies
- ☐ Soap
- ☐ Crisps

- ☐ Cleaning products
- ☐ Toothpaste
- ☐ Pizza bases
- ☐ Ice cream
- ☐ Instant noodles

The answer is – all of them!

It's hard to know which products use palm oil because it is sometimes called by another name. So keep the following list handy and next time your family goes shopping, check the ingredients. Avoid buying products that contain:

- anything with the word 'palm' in it
- cetyl alcohol
- cetyl palmitate
- elaeis guineensis
- emulsifiers 422, 430–36, 470–8, 481–3, 493–5
- glyceryl stearate
- octyl palmitate
- palm fruit oil
- palm kernel oil
- palm stearine
- palmate/palmitate
- palmitic acid
- palmityl alcohol
- palmolein
- sodium dodecyl sulfate
- sodium kernelate
- sodium laureth / lauryl sulfate
- sodium lauryl lactylate
- sodium lauryl sulfoacetate
- stearate
- steareth 2 & 20
- stearic acid
- vegetable glycerin
- vegetable oil
- vitamin A palmitate

EAT FEWER ANIMAL PRODUCTS

How you shop for food is actually one of the most powerful ways you can fight animal cruelty. Start by reducing the amount of meat, eggs and dairy products you eat. Think about the animals that produced your food, which means choosing the meat carefully and making sure it has come from a good place where the animals were treated well.

Here are some tips for making positive changes to your diet – check your progress as you try them!

* Make the changes slowly. Experiment with being a vegetarian one or two days a week and see how you go.

* Work out which vegetables you like the most and make them the star of your meal.

* Consider drinking other kinds of milk, such as soy, rice and almond or other nut milks. Just make sure these other milks have added calcium to ensure you have healthy bones.

* If your school has a canteen, encourage them to provide more meat-free options, and to avoid factory-farmed egg and meat products. Get your friends and family on board too.

* Remember to keep an open mind about all the different foods you can try.

HOW TO EAT LESS MEAT

If you decide to eat less meat and dairy, chat with a grown-up first. It's important to eat more foods that contain vitamin D, calcium, protein, iron and omega-3 fatty acids. If you're cutting out animal products, you may also need to take vitamin B12 supplements. Here are some other foods you could eat more of to ensure you get the nutrition you need:

VITAMIN D – Mushrooms and almond milk with added vitamin D. Get a little sunlight.

CALCIUM – Calcium-set tofu, sesame seeds, dried fruit, fortified foods like soy and almond milk, almonds, greens like kale, bok choy and broccoli.

PROTEIN – Beans, lentils, chickpeas, nuts, quinoa, chia seeds, tofu, oats, wild rice, soy milk.

IRON – Lentils, tofu, quinoa, brown rice, oatmeal, pumpkin, cashew nuts, spinach, prune juice.

OMEGA 3 – Chia seeds, hemp seeds, kidney beans, brussel sprouts, walnuts, seaweed, blueberries, wild rice.

TALK FOR THE ANIMALS

Animals can't speak for themselves. So you have to be the voices for creatures who can't ask for help when they need it. If you see animal abuse, report it. If you see an injured animal, don't just leave it – take it to a vet.

Animal welfare organisations recommend these three steps:

1 If you have found a sick, injured or orphaned animal, remove any threat to the animal. This includes keeping all people and pets away to minimise stress to the animal until vet transport or a rescuer arrives.

2 If it is safe to do so, contain the animal in a warm, dark, quiet place. For example, gently wrap the animal in a towel and place it in a ventilated box with a lid, then transport it carefully to the nearest vet or wait for a rescuer to arrive.

3 Do not give the animal any food or water, unless instructed to by a vet or the RSPCA.

Another way you can speak up for animals is to write a letter to your MP (Member of Parliament) or to a newspaper, saying why you are worried about the treatment of animals.

Remember to use positive encouragement – this means explaining why changes will be good for animals, rather than focusing on why what people are doing is bad.

Write your letter here.

RAISING AWARENESS

Is there an environmental problem that you really care about? Is something unfair? Does it make you angry? Then tell people about it and get people on your side!

The more people know about an issue, the better. Learn as much as you can about issues that are important to you. For example, maybe you are particularly passionate about some of the things you have read about in this book:

* plastic pollution
* ethical fashion
* reducing waste
* the meat, egg and fishing industries
* organic food
* saving energy and water
* animal welfare

Once you've found out the facts, educate your friends and family about the issue. You can start a petition online to raise awareness and make a change, or write a letter to a newspaper. Spread the word and help others learn about the issue too. Get people talking about the issue in your community. Do what you can to help the people involved in the cause.

KIDS WHO CHANGED THE WORLD

Greta Thunberg

Greta Thunberg was 15 years old when she started protesting outside the Swedish parliament. She feels that much more must be done to stop global warming. Her passionate protests made her world-famous and made many people sit up and listen. She appeared on the cover of *Time* magazine and was talked about as a possible recipient of the Nobel Peace Prize. In 2019, she addressed the UN Climate Action Summit in New York.

SAVE-THE-WORLD SUPERHERO

You're on the way to saving the world yourself, but what if you had some help? What if there was a superhero who loved saving the planet? Well, let's create one! Answer these questions to help you create a cool new planet-saving superhero.

* What is your superhero's name?

* What powers do they have?

* Where do they live?

* What is their alter-ego?

* What is their costume like?

* Who is their arch-enemy?

* Think of a time when they come to the rescue. Who do they save?

* What dangers do they face?

* How do they finally win?

Draw your 'Save-the-World Superhero'.

AN ACT OF KINDNESS

Saving the planet doesn't only mean helping the natural world and its plants and animals. It also means making a difference to the lives of the people around you. Choose to be kind to people, because sometimes the world can be unkind. Besides, being nice has been scientifically proven to be good for you too. Kindness boosts something in our bodies called serotonin, which makes us feel happier and more positive.

Sometimes it's difficult to be nice when you are feeling down, but it's always best to try. You might even start to feel better yourself – any act of kindness, no matter how big or small, helps your family, friends, the people around you, the environment and the world.

The world can be a difficult place for many people, whether it's because they are elderly, sick, poor, homeless, lonely, unhappy, or just having a bad day.

Practise being nice in these simple ways every day

- Smile at people. Smiling makes everyone feel better.

- Always say 'Good morning'.

- Listen when people are talking to you before responding. People enjoy talking about themselves!

- Give someone a compliment.

- Hold the door for someone.

- Offer your seat to someone on public transport.

- Say 'Hi' to someone at school who you don't usually talk to.

- Try to understand how others are feeling. This is called empathy.

- If someone looks upset, ask if they are okay.

- Help people when they are struggling. If a relative has lots to do, offer your support.

- Do a chore without being asked, and without telling anyone.

- Thank people when they do something nice for you.

- Make breakfast for your family, or help a friend or sibling with their homework.

- Remember to be kind to yourself too.

Now think of a way of your own to be kind to people:

This week I will

RAISE MONEY

When it comes to raising money for charity or good causes, every single penny counts. No matter how much you raise, people will be so glad that you helped them. So how can you actually raise money?

It could be as simple as baking some flapjacks to sell or setting up a lemonade stand. Or if you are good at something else, such as sewing, knitting, pottery, art, making jewellery or woodwork, you can sell the things you make to raise money.

But you don't **have** to be super-skilful at something. If you go to the trouble of making an effort, people will be happy to sponsor you.

Anyone can wash cars – all it takes is soap, water and a sponge – and there are probably plenty of people in your street who would pay to have a clean car!

GET SPONSORED

What could you and your friends do to raise some money for your favourite cause? Write your ideas down here. And here's a sample letter to help you.

Dear <space for person's name>

On the <date> of <month> I am going to <activity>. This will take a lot of effort but it will be worth it because I want to raise money for <your cause>.

I would be very grateful if you could sponsor me to do this. Even 50p per <lap or activity> would make a big difference to <an example of your cause, such as the orangutans of Indonesia>.

Thank you!
<your name>

JOIN AN ORGANISATION

Your voice will be even louder if you join a like-minded organisation. Here are some that share your thinking about saving the planet.

GREENPEACE (greenpeace.org.uk)
Greenpeace describes climate change as 'the number one threat facing our planet' and is famous for taking direct action.

FRIENDS OF THE EARTH (foei.org)
This organisation describes itself as a 'bold and fearless voice for justice and the planet'. It has targeted bee-killing pesticides and palm oil production.

RAINFOREST ALLIANCE (rainforest-alliance.org)
They make sure that rainforest products, such as chocolate, coffee, bananas and tea, are produced in a way that doesn't harm the environment.

UNION OF CONCERNED SCIENTISTS (ucsusa.org)
This is a network of nearly 17,000 scientists who believe 'rigorous analysis is the best way to understand the world's pressing problems and develop effective solutions to them'.

WORLD WILDLIFE FUND (wwf.org.uk)
They are dedicated to 'building a future in which human needs are met in harmony with nature'.

1% FOR THE PLANET (onepercentfortheplanet.org)
They help companies be greener by giving back to environmental causes.

NATIONAL GEOGRAPHIC SOCIETY (nationalgeographic.org)
This organisation is one of the oldest and largest green groups.

SAVE THE CHILDREN (savethechildren.net)
They are dedicated to improving the lives of children around the world through better education, health care and opportunities.

RSPB (rspb.org.uk)
The Royal Society for the Protection of Birds has been protecting birds since 1889 and is the largest nature conservation charity in the country.

DREAM BIG

Grown-ups might have more knowledge than you, but they also might be stuck in their ways of thinking. Sometimes it takes a fresh viewpoint – and a young mind – to think of a brilliant new idea.

Use this space to write down or sketch out some really big planet-saving ideas.

START NOW

You are never too young to start making a difference. A journey of a thousand miles starts with one step. So even by doing something small today – helping an animal, recycling plastic, or talking about the environment – you are on your way to saving the planet.

DID YOU KNOW?

Louis Braille was only 15 years old when he invented braille, a system of reading and writing for the blind or visually impaired.

Elizabeth Rintels was 12 when she won the grand prize in a Going Green Challenge with a smart device that measures and monitors water use in the shower.

'Whatever you can do or dream you can, begin it.

Boldness has genius, power, and magic in it.'

Johann Wolfgang von Goethe,
famous playwright and thinker

Published by Collins
An imprint of HarperCollins Publishers
Westerhill Road, Bishopbriggs, Glasgow, G64 2QT

www.harpercollins.co.uk

Material first published by Pantera Press as You Can Change the World © 2019 Lucy Bell
Text © Lucy Bell
Images © Shutterstock.com

Publisher: Michelle I'Anson
Project manager: Rachel Allegro
Design: Sarah Duxbury
Typesetter: Jouve
Text editor: Richard Happer
Cover: Kevin Robbins

9780008374563

Printed in China

10 9 8 7 6 5 4 3 2 1